WRITERS

ON

WRITERS

Published in partnership with

WRITERS
SARAH
KRASNOSTEIN
ON
PETER
CAREY
WRITERS

Published by Black Inc.
in association with the University of Melbourne and State Library Victoria.

Black Inc., an imprint of Schwartz Books Pty Ltd
22–24 Northumberland Street, Collingwood VIC 3066, Australia
enquiries@blackincbooks.com
www.blackincbooks.com

State Library Victoria
328 Swanston Street, Melbourne Victoria 3000 Australia
www.slv.vic.gov.au

The University of Melbourne
Parkville Victoria 3010 Australia
www.unimelb.edu.au

9781760643904 (hardback)
9781743823095 (ebook)

A catalogue record for this
book is available from the
National Library of Australia

Cover design by Peter Long and Akiko Chan
Typesetting by Typography Studio
Photograph of Sarah Krasnostein: Gina Milicia
Photograph of Peter Carey: Heike Steinweg

Printed in China by 1010 Printing.

I wish to acquaint you with some of the occurrences of the present past and future.

Ned Kelly, The Jerilderie Letter (1879)

I take her hand, wishing to reassure her. It removes itself from her body. I am talking to her. Touching her, wishing that she should answer me. But with each touch she is dismembered, slowly, limb by limb. Until, headless, armless, legless, I carelessly lose my grip and she falls to the floor. There is a sharp noise, rather like breaking glass.

Bending down I discover among the fragments a small doll, hairless, eyeless, and white from head to toe.

Peter Carey, 'Peeling',
in The Fat Man in History (1974)

Thank you, Your Majesty, for everything.

Peter Dutton, 'Statement on the Death of
Queen Elizabeth II', 9 September 2022

PROLOGUE

The first-edition University of Queensland Press paperback of Peter Carey's *True History of the Kelly Gang* sat on my bookshelf for nearly twenty years, unread, its cover slowly bleaching in the light through a succession of ever-changing windows. I moved ten times in that period, and wherever I unpacked my increasingly decrepit Ikea bookshelf and its contents, there it was – with its alienating ochres and inscrutable colonial maps and bizarre bushrangers, whoever they were. The book's pleasingly ironic title and double Booker / triple Miles Franklin–winning author were enough for me to keep it, but not enough to draw me in. A couple of years ago, I cracked it open and started reading. I couldn't stop. And then I couldn't stop talking about it.

*

Well before his corpse lay in the deadhouse of Melbourne Gaol, minds differed on the moral valence of Ned Kelly. Context was ignored, knowledge forgotten. Those who met him felt something that those reading about him in the newspapers didn't. We continue to disagree, and strongly. This ambivalence – what Carl Jung referred to as the tension of opposites – generates much of the energy that keeps Kelly's story alive. But beneath that split moves something deeper, which is responsible for the sustained emotional force of this passage of our history; something gestured towards by the facts, which remain as incomplete as his headless skeleton, buried only recently in consecrated ground.

If you look closely at what is known about Kelly's short life, they're all there: the scrounging labourers; the imported livestock more protected than people; the altitudinous squatters and their troopers one two three; the suicidal defiance of unjust authority; the ghosts whispering on stolen land and waterways. It's 'Waltzing Matilda', with its tropes of the empire's most distant colony, but not as they usually hit – with their heroes and villains so polished into caricature we can't see them straight.

Three Victorian policemen hunting the Kelly Gang were killed by them at Stringybark Creek in 1878. When Ned was killed by the state two years later for the murder of two of them, the creak of the rope round his neck was the last note in a long song. But the novelist's obsession is not with how things end. The novelist's preoccupation is that of the historian and the lawyer and the judge and the detective and the psychologist and the child: *Why?* Don't bet on their answers being the same.

*

Like the most credible testimony, and the most powerful fiction, Kelly's Jerilderie Letter speaks – as Carey's novels typically do – in the first person. The letter was written around the start of 1879, before

Kelly rode into the town of that name with his brother Dan, his mates Joe Byrne and Steve Hart, and an enormous bounty on his head, offered to whoever could put a bullet in it – no warning to surrender necessary. 'A Policeman is a disgrace to his country,' Kelly dictated to Byrne, 'not alone to the mother that suckled him, in the first place he is a rogue in his heart but too cowardly to follow it up without having the force to disguise it.'

*

'There are doubtless as many good policemen as there are good bushrangers,' wrote Sidney Nolan – whose grandfather and great-grandfather were mounted Victorian policemen – in 1948, after he had embarked on his Ned Kelly series, twenty-seven painted panels of the figure and the ground. The Ern Malley affair had shown him the way in, inspired him to 'take the risk of putting against the Australian bush an utterly strange object'.[1]

*

In his pamphlet on the revered colonial judge Redmond Barry, Peter Ryan argued that the elevation of Kelly to hero status was a perverse signifier of 'the corrosive envy, the black defeated nothingness that lie somewhere near the heart of the Australian character'.[2]

What could Ryan have meant by that nothingness near the heart? I wonder whether he was inspired by Louis Joseph Vance's 1907 hard-boiled detective story, *The Brass Bowl,* in which a young woman stares wide-eyed 'into the black heart of nothingness, until the night seemed pricked with evanescent periods of dim fire, peopled with monstrous and terrible shadows closing about her … Yet – it was absurd! She must not yield to such puerile superstitions. There was nothing there … There *was* something there … something that like an incarnation of hatred was stalking her.'

Psychoanalysts have spent lifetimes telling us that when it comes to the heart, nothing is always something.

*

The grainy footage didn't diminish the thrilling immediacy of hearing Jung speak in the interview I watched online. 'When you observe the world,' he said, his voice pressing out from the past, 'you see people, you see houses, you see the sky – you see tangible objects. But when you observe yourself within, you [also] see … a world of images – generally known as fantasies. Yet these fantasies are *facts*. Indeed … it is such a tangible fact, for instance, that when a man has a certain fantasy, another man may lose his life.'

*

In Australia we recently had a public holiday to mourn the Queen's death. An *Age* poll showed that most respondents would put King Charles on the five-dollar note, well ahead of Uncle Archie Roach or Uncle Jack Charles. It's not time to discuss becoming a republic. According to our newspapers, it's time to discuss 'The lesser known royals in the spotlight following the Queen's death' and 'What has art predicted for King Charles' reign' and displacing the Aboriginal name of Maroondah Hospital with the Queen's name as 'a mark of respect' and 'the steadfast silence of a determined people' lining up along the Thames with 'a patient resoluteness that seems almost a throwback to another age'.

*

'I wanted to deal ironically with the cliche of the "dead heart",' Nolan explained of his work. 'I wanted to know the true nature of the "otherness" I had been born into. It was not a European thing. I wanted to paint the great purity and implacability of the landscape. I wanted a visual form of the "otherness" of the thing not seen.'[3]

*

'I have the good fortune,' Carey told *The Paris Review* in 2006, 'that my own personal trauma matches my country's great historical trauma.'

I

In 1943, when Peter Carey was born in the small town of Bacchus Marsh, 53 kilometres west of Melbourne, Australians were British subjects, not yet recognised as citizens of their own country. Had Ned Kelly lived long like his mother, he would've been eighty-eight that year. His brother Jim was still living near the original Kelly selection at Eleven Mile Creek in north-eastern Victoria, where family shielded him from press and other visitors.[4] 'Many lies have been written about Ned Kelly,' a relative said. 'It is no good going back into the past and asking the old man for his memories.'

Sidney Nolan was twenty-six. He had unsuccessfully sought patronage from Keith Murdoch to further his studies, then found with it the Reeds – John and Sunday – before being interrupted by full-time duty in the Citizen Military Forces. He was posted with an army supply company in the far western Victorian town of Nhill. The war meant a serious shortage of farmhands in the Wimmera, and the weather meant that a good fall of rain was needed to spring the grass. Surrounded by that parched vastness, Nolan searched for 'the constant beneath' the shifting appearance of the landscape. Some way of capturing 'the quality of space and distance' that he could not yet satisfactorily see or paint.[5]

For the next few years, Carey and Nolan and the youngest Kelly shared a time and a state. Three white males of Irish heritage. British subjects on stolen land. Separated by a few hundred kilometres, their beating hearts, if plotted on a map, would have formed a shaky isosceles triangle. I had this strange shape in my mind as I went looking for something I wasn't confident could be seen, driving from Melbourne to Bacchus Marsh, where the clouds looked like Nolan painted them in *Ned Kelly* (1946) – so low it seemed possible to touch them from the elevation of a saddle.

*

Like I said, I was a bit slow coming to Carey. If I was reading about Melbourne, I was reading Helen Garner. If I was reading about Australia, I was reading Alexis Wright. And if I was breathing, I was reading – Auden and Munro and Bellow and Bulgakov and Baldwin, Malcolm and Márquez and Morrison and McPhee and Kundera. When it came to Carey, I think my reluctance had nothing to do with him per se and everything to do with an unarticulated, to myself, perceptual shorthand busily protecting me from a feeling of utter depletion when it came to the historical fictions of certain older Australian men.

My passion for Australian history is fairly recent. It dates from around the time I started feeling at home here. By which I mean: in my relationships and my body and my work and my house, more than the land they're on, which never was and never will be mine. Feeling truly at home here requires one to look at such things directly.

*

For many years, I thought the opening line of Gabriel García Márquez's *One Hundred Years of Solitude* could not be bettered for perspective and propulsion: 'Many years later, as he faced the firing squad, Colonel Aureliano Buendía was to remember that distant afternoon when his father took him to discover ice.' But then I started *True History*.

> I lost my own father at 12 yr. of age and know what it is to be raised on lies and silences my dear daughter you are presently too young to understand a word I write but this history is for you and will contain no single lie may I burn in Hell if I speak false.

Unlike Márquez, who was left as a newborn to be raised by his grandparents, Carey spent his first eleven years with his parents in Bacchus Marsh. Then he was sent to board at Geelong Grammar. Both opening lines, however, are about fathers and children, reaching towards someone who is absent, the past in the present.

*

'I was a bit slow in coming to Dickens for all sorts of reasons,' Carey said in a 1997 interview promoting *Jack Maggs*, after Ramona Koval, his interlocutor, noted that he once called *Great Expectations* a perfect novel.[6] 'Dickens' life was interesting to me,' Carey continued, 'and there were all sorts of things that any writer reading about another writer could identify with.' These included 'a lot of energy', money worries and a peculiar, brutal striving.

He was always wanting to be loved, and I don't think this is my major psychosis or anything like that, but you can see that to greater and lesser extents writers' relationships with their audiences are often ... you know. If you are a writer you go out on a cold night and no-one even knows who you are. Dickens at the end of his life went on this huge reading tour with this special reading stand that he had built with these lights at the top and a special lectern that he used to assemble at every place, and he killed himself doing this but what he got from that tour were these huge crowds and all these people loving him and given his feelings of neglect and abandonment as a child, I always found that very interesting.

When I read this, it felt as though something exploded in my chest. I have this unvoiced feeling less frequently these days. But I felt it the first time I read the line of which Carey's description of Dickens reminded me: Auden's 'recipe for the upbringing of a poet: As much neurosis as the child can bear'.

*

'At 1st we would shout out to him,' Ned Kelly remembers at the start of *True History*, about his father who was gaoled for the last time before dying from alcoholism when Ned was twelve, 'but never got any answer and finally we all give up excepting Jem who runs his hands along the frost cold walls patting the prison like a dog.' On reading it: that explosion. A real book – Auden again – is not one that we read, but one that reads us.

*

An English friend of Carey's who had recently finished *Jack Maggs* told him about passing the Seven Dials in London, a setting in the novel, and being excited to recognise it. Carey explained: 'And I suddenly realised that he was carrying in his head a huge London that he could apply to my book, and my London was a much smaller London, little corners here and there, but it could connect with his bigger London ... [T]ogether through that wonderful thing that happens in reading, he got this big world.'

Nolan once wrote to the artist John Perceval that '[t]echnically there is no such thing as a continuous vision, we are not constituted that way, one flash succeeds another; it is our job to preserve that one organic and spontaneous moment of vision and at the same time make the necessary artifices of language that constitute communication'.[7]

An author is looking for the person who connects the dots, fills the white space, sees herself in the pages, 'every word lead[ing] her, by one course or another ... to her own situation': their reader.[8] And once the book has found its reader, it has found its home, and become one.

Home is one of Carey's central themes. In the unfurling of certain lives, reality impels us to revisit our notion of home. To look at it directly and honestly, or to refuse that call and double down on our compensatory myths or lies or half-truths. This is when things start to get interesting. I'm fascinated by the homes Carey builds, and the one he inherited.

*

Carey came up in the early 1970s, frenetically writing failed novels while living in London, then submitting short stories to newspapers and magazines with increasing success until he broke through, at thirty-three, with the collection *The Fat Man in History* (1974) and another one, *War Crimes* (1979). After *Bliss* (1981), his first published novel, his characters – particularly the women – grew rounder, deeper. *Illywhacker* (1985) was followed by *Oscar & Lucinda* (1988). After relocating to New York, he published *The Tax Inspector* (1991), *The Unusual Life of Tristan Smith* (1994), *Jack Maggs* (1997), *True History of the Kelly Gang* (2000), *My Life as a Fake* (2003), *Theft: A Love Story* (2006),

His Illegal Self (2008), *Parrot and Olivier in America* (2009), *The Chemistry of Tears* (2012), *Amnesia* (2014) and *A Long Way from Home* (2017). A three-year cycle, give or take, which is remarkable given his work's quality and complexity.

He's 'always always always' thought of himself as a political writer.[9] With *Bliss*, he was said to have predicted the 'Me Generation' of the 1980s. With *Parrot and Olivier*, he was said to have predicted Trump's presidency. Promoting *Amnesia* in 2015 – before the rise of the Black Lives Matter, Me Too and Extinction Rebellion movements – he spoke about what political action would look like in the future. 'The people who are kids now are going to be, and are now already, a lot more politically involved and active than we've thought, and will perhaps be doing things that we would once have thought of as extreme because they think that … the crisis for humanity is huge, and none of the institutions are really going to address them. You're going to find people like [one of *Amnesia*'s protagonists]

Gaby who think it's their moral responsibility to act. I just think that's where we are.'

Frequently, through intergenerational monologues (protagonists explaining to their children; descendants explaining their forebears; that ever-explaining, ruminating 'I'), he decants the enormous sweep of colonial history into finely observed domestic details, serving it up on a human scale. His themes: the violence pulsing just below the skin of good order; outsiders, outcasts and orphans; shame and its defences; betrayal; risk; denial and other contortions that the psyche performs to avoid threats to its preferred self-concept. Also: something I could reduce to the words 'freedom' or 'joy', but which is more accurately described as a life-enlarging wonder untethered to the maw into which one has been delivered. I believe this is what W.G. Sebald (whose *Austerlitz*, with its emulsion of fact and fiction, Carey admires greatly) meant by the quality of 'lightness': 'not that the narrator is carefree or light-hearted; but instead of talking about his burdens, he turns to his senses in order to produce something that can help him and his reader, who may also be in need of comfort, to resist the temptation of melancholy'.[10] I should also mention that Carey is a deft humourist; he knows where the funny is, as Sheila Heti once put it in an entirely different context.

He is a master craftsman. He can flip an omniscient third-person perspective into an intimate first with the flick of a letter-writing quill. He can hoist aloft hilariously low material on the lever of an elegant nineteenth-century sentence structure. He is surprising, at times so devastatingly tender he can kill you with a line no longer than a needle. My highest praise: remembering that a Carey novel is waiting by my chair or at my bedside always gladdens me, and has been of comfort. I have never felt lonely while reading them.

*

Boat against the current, Carey is borne back ceaselessly. But from what he has said publicly, this eternal return does not apply to his personal history. He told Koval, when she asked whether criticism of his work had ever yielded valuable insights:

Occasionally, I've read things that illuminated patterns in my work – of abandonment, orphans – and made me recognise that where this pattern came in from my life was probably the trauma of going to boarding school, which I had never thought was a trauma. I mean, I was the happy camper: a lot of energy and enthusiasm and getting on with it. The homesick kid was that kid over there weeping in the corner; it was never me. And so, finally, reading somebody else writing about my work, I recognised what the psychological roots of some of my invention were, that I continued to have orphans and

I continued to have abandoned children and so on.

Having seen that, I really don't think it helps me. In fact, I felt a little less strong and less powerful for knowing it; self-consciousness was not helping me there. So, I like to say to my friends in New York, who are all totally committed to their therapists, I like to say to them that the unexamined life is the only one worth living, and I get a cheap laugh out of it, I suppose.

'I wonder,' Koval asked, 'if someone who has your sort of imagination dreams at all or if you just pour all of your unconscious life into your books.'

'I think it's the latter,' Carey replied. 'I mostly no longer remember my dreams.'

*

Ned Kelly 'wanted land and horses, and a place where he could exist', Carey explained to *The New*

York Times when *True History* came out. 'And of course that's me. All my books are full of people wanting homes.'[11]

'Really, the Kelly paintings are secretly about myself,' Sidney Nolan told the artist and writer Elwyn Lynn in the 1960s. 'You would be surprised if I told you … It's an inner history of my own emotions.'[12]

*

Carey was born in Australia and moved to America in 1991, when he was in his forties. I was born in America and moved to Australia in 1994, when I was in my teens. Despite telephones and planes, moving continents involved a great haemorrhaging of people and places. With moves of that magnitude, words are the next to go. First vocabulary, then inflection. This is followed by a reflexive confidence with space and time – cultural references, historical context, directions, units of measurement, seasons. Even when these are re-mastered and proprioception is restored, distance remains the perpetual problem.

Asked why he continued to set most of his books in Australia, Carey recalled one of his students saying that when you change countries you lose your peripheral vision. 'I left Bacchus Marsh when I was eleven,' he said, in another interview, 'and it's been twenty years since I lived in Bellingen – I was astonished by how clearly I could see lost places.'[13]

*

True History was not the first book Carey wrote after moving to the States. But it may be accurate to say it was the first book he wrote when the move began to seem permanent.

In 2007, ahead of the release of *His Illegal Self*, he was interviewed by *The Courier-Mail* for a profile entitled 'Yearning for Home'. 'He has spent nearly two decades living in New York, but says one never loses a sense of being Australian.

"People tend to think you do and also, I realise now, that I've got a kid who was born here who is 17. So I've been here 17, almost 18 years. In my mind it's not like that at all."'

*

Carey's books are full of warm rooms and their opposites. Oscar's dormitory at Oriel, for instance, 'so bare' with the 'cold empty space between objects', 'nothing familiar, nothing one would expect at home, no port on the mantel, no rugs … no fire in the grate'.[14] Or Lucinda visiting the vicar of Woollahra and 'falling asleep in the leather armchair beside the fire', her hands around a warm mug, 'wishing only that she did not have to travel the moon-pale clay tracks to her hotel'.[15] Jack Maggs trespassing in the master's house, drowsily breathing its 'strange yet familiar' English smells, 'polished oak, coal dust, Devon apples'. Little Ned Kelly with his mum, 'drenched to the bone' at Beveridge Police Camp: 'a strong odour about us like wet dogs and for this or other reasons we was excluded from the Sergeant's room. I remember sitting with my chilblained hands wedged beneath the door I could feel the lovely warmth of the fire on my fingertips.'

*

I am a fourth-generation American and a third-generation Australian. When I arrived in Australia, the country, like the relatives residing here, was largely unknown to me. The calendar behaved differently. Traditions died in their sleep. Holidays passed like any other day, replaced by others unfreighted with meaning – 'of no significance at all'.[16]

I have trouble answering the question, 'Where are you from?' and have learned to distance myself from the rising discomfort it elicits inside me with a joke: 'Nowhere.' Take my accent. To the Aussie ear – mostly American. To the American ear – frequently alien. Often I'm uncertain in the moment which word or pronunciation belongs to which continent. My personal vernacular is a hybrid of two Englishes and the effect recalls John Stuart Mill's derision of the word 'sociology', with its mixed Latin and Greek etymology, as 'a convenient barbarism'. In each country, I make mistakes which spark good-natured laughter or honest confusion. And when this happens, a part of me freezes – panicked, ashamed – instantly returned to the wrong side of the threshold to that warm room.

Carey was not moved, but rather chose to plant himself on American soil – as an act of agency or adventure or accommodation or aspiration. But still, mutatis mutandis, when Carey speaks, I feel that I recognise another barbarian, and perhaps something else besides. 'Yes, we tend to be self-taught,' Carey answered once when asked about his lack of formal training, 'and there's a part of me that thinks that's the way it should be – you do it alone, you learn to endure loneliness.'

For the longest time – before my husband and I created the warm place where I will soon down tools and step into my real life 'strong and bright and solid'[17] – my home was on the page, writing, reading, always having near me 'the splash of eggshell-white from the open heart of a book'.[18] There, I truly belonged to what Hélène Cixous described as 'a fantastical nation which is that of literature'.[19] What I'm trying to say is that I understand what it is to write oneself into that somewhere space that exists nowhere as concrete as an address, but rather where longing itself pulses, just beneath the clavicle.

II

I n 1802, Matthew Flinders described the western plains where Woiwuruung Country met Wathaurong Country as 'grassy and very slightly covered with wood, presenting great facility to a traveller desirous of penetrating inland'.[20] Carey's early life in Bacchus Marsh, the town that sprouted nearby three decades later, resembles one of his novels – full of quirky characters meeting modernity, a mix of the mundane and the magical and the menacing.

His maternal grandparents were teachers. His paternal grandmother once won the 'Shortest Woman' award in a beach contest. His paternal grandfather – Irish – was a pilot, holding Australia's first commercial flying permit, delivering its first airmail. In 1948, Carey's parents purchased the town's garage and car dealership from the family who had sold many of the area's first cars. Like his older siblings, he attended the local primary school, Victoria's oldest state school, where the magpies swooped the children of miners and farmers and shopkeepers as they raced to the dunny and back. There, Carey was immersed in the vernacular he spun across 389 pages in *True History*. 'Although the vocabulary has changed a little,' he once explained, 'the 1940s had more in common with the 1870s than they do with now in terms of the language and beliefs.'[21]

*

There is a photo of Ned's mother, Ellen Kelly, at the wheel of a car shortly before she died, faster than any horse she ever rode, and more lethal. It still shocks me.

*

To understand how small a country town was when Carey was born, you must first understand how small was the city it orbited. You could place an ad in *The Age* with some reasonable hope of finding your lost pay packet or your wedding ring or your white cow or your spectacles or your false teeth or a single blue woollen glove. There was agreement among the newspapers' target audience about who 'the Enemy' was. The Germans were feared. The Japanese were feared. 'Atheism and irreligion' were feared. In the newspapers, as on the streets, faces were predominantly white, names mostly Anglo.

Those newspapers could not imagine that a tram driver's son would paint images of Ned Kelly worthy of 'stand[ing] alone in any gallery anywhere in the world'.[22] Or that a kid from Bacchus Marsh Primary would one day take as his muses orphans, convicts and Kelly himself to win one of Britain's greatest literary prizes – twice.

*

Modernity is usually dated from around the late eighteenth century. But in a sense Carey's childhood was pre-modern. One knew one's neighbours, one's place. Interior life was continuous. The church had a monopoly on morality and respectability. Violence was, falsely or otherwise, explicated or plausibly denied.

Carey Motors opened a few doors down from the school before moving to the corner of Main and Grant, where it served the local community until 1987. His mother, Helen, managed the business. His older siblings worked there. His father, Percy, was referred to in a 1955 General Motors handbook as 'tomorrow-minded' with 'an unblemished reputation for fair-dealing', a man who enjoyed telling how on the coldest day for fifty years, with snow falling, he cornered a farmer in a field and sold him a refrigerator. Carey would remember his father, who left school at fourteen, standing by the window in his pyjamas at three a.m., worrying about the cars he needed to sell. How they read the same Biggles books on holidays, his father flipping to the end to make sure everything turned out okay. 'He did business in pubs and became an alcoholic,' Carey has said. 'He was never unpleasant or violent, but he was continually pissed.'

Carey would be one of the few boys at Geelong Grammar with 'a working mother', both Depression-era parents labouring to pay the astronomical cost of providing 'something better' for their baby, whom they entrusted during the school term to the care of one of the most elite schools in the country, founded in 1855 under the auspices of the Church of England.

'I suppose it did solve a few child-care problems,' Carey told *The Paris Review*, of boarding at the school from 1954 to 1960. 'I never felt I was being exiled or sent away, but I was only eleven years old. No one could have guessed that the experience would finally produce an endless string of orphan characters in my books.'

Carey spoke about the school, between songs from his adolescence, on the BBC's *Desert Island*

Discs. He described 'playing hooky' at seventeen with a mate, smoking and listening to Miles Davis and John Coltrane on a veranda, imagining his future in a city he couldn't yet name. He mentioned how the Elvis records he'd buy during breaks back home were the wrong Elvis records. The sweaters he wore were the wrong sweaters. And then he described something as being the flipside to that feeling of never quite belonging.

'In Bacchus Marsh,' he told the host, 'it would be impossible to imagine Handel's *Messiah*. Geelong Grammar had what I thought a hugely grand chapel … And every year, as I recall, they'd do something like the *Messiah* and it was thrilling for me, as a child from Bacchus Marsh, to go into the chapel with all these beautiful voices of these boys, to listen to the "Hallelujah Chorus". Now it's like an enormous musical *Mona Lisa* cliché,' he said, with a distancing chuckle, 'and yet if one tries really hard to get beyond that, I certainly still feel the sheer soaring glory of it.'

Carey's elite education contained 'one memorable year' when the fourteen- and fifteen-year-old Grammarians 'were sent upstate to live in the bush at an outward bound school in the foothills of Mount Buller, a place called Timbertop'.[23] This is also King Charles's and Kerry Packer's and Rupert Murdoch's alma mater, located in the High Country, the landscape of *True History*.

Carey graduated having read nothing that inspired him to read further, let alone write. But once he gathered momentum, he would write books that burned down houses like Geelong Grammar, and those of the old boys who prospered by them.

*

Carey's books are not seen as radical today. And perhaps – given their popularity, both here and in the UK – they never were. Indeed, it's possible to misread them as rollicking yarns, studded with recognisable tropes of Mother England and her most distant colony. But he is always writing towards our 'Great Amnesia' in all its permutations. Take *Oscar & Lucinda,* which won the Booker before *Mabo* was decided. Its central image is a glass house of Christian stories – as alien as it is brittle – floating precariously through a land of Aboriginal stories.[24] In that novel, Carey conjures the enabling hypocrisies of the religious settlers who thought cribbage a sin while turning their backs on the state-sanctioned murder of men, women and children.[25] 'The stories of the gospel lay across the harsh landscape like sheets of newspaper on a polished floor. They slid, slipped, did not connect to anything beneath them.'[26] And he evokes the drives of those capitalising on the colony in its early days: 'Sometimes he thought of Sydney as an orphan's party with a dressing-up box.'[27]

He has referred to 'the complete ease with which [Australians] have accepted corruption since (and perhaps because of) the first white settlement in Sydney Cove', emphasised that 'we are a barely postcolonial culture' and described Whitlam's time in office as an unseized opportunity for 'fairness and decency' – the time when 'we could have the courage not to be a client state'.[28] *Amnesia* skewers those who normalised punitive politicking, from the Whitlam dismissal to Howard's refugee policy:

> The fourth estate made a whole country believe the refugees were animals and swine. Many think so still. Yet the refugees belonged here. They would have been at home with the best of us. We have a history of courage and endurance, of inventiveness in the face of isolation and moral threat. At the same time, alas, we have displayed this awful level of cowardice, brown-nosing, criminality, mediocrity and nest-feathering.[29]

'When my country began the European phase of its history there had already been some fifty thousand years of Aboriginal settlement,' Carey said, while promoting *Jack Maggs*. 'We grew up denying it, of course. Certainly it never occurred to us that the land was stolen, or that we had anything to do with the agony of the transported convicts. When we imagined who we were, we somehow imagined ourselves on the soldier's end of the whip. I wanted to write about this false consciousness for a long, long time.'

*

After graduating from high school, Carey started a science degree at the new Monash University. In *Amnesia*, Felix – one of '347 freshmen at Monash University' – would remember that '[t]here had been no second- or third- or fourth-year students. Indeed there had not been a Monash University the year before … I had no conscious knowledge of why I had chosen a university with no cloisters, no quadrangles, no suck-up colleges, no private school boys with their Triumph TR3s. Instead I had chosen the sea of mud that had been a market garden, where the footpaths were not yet paved.'[30] The course fitted Carey's interests so poorly that he felt grateful when injuries sustained in a serious car accident provided an immediate excuse not to continue.

Leaving after one year, he began what would become a sustaining career in advertising. This elicited a revulsion from his uni friends which could be ameliorated by the supplementary information that he was working on a novel. And it was true. Influenced by the literary cohort of ad men at his day job, he had started reading – devouring – in earnest: Beckett, Faulkner, Joyce, Kafka, Márquez. And that was when he started writing.

*

In a 2004 interview with the BBC, Carey discussed the nation's antecedents as a penal colony:

> I don't know why foundation stories continue to leach through into the present. But I have

sort of a notion about why it mattered to the Australians of that time. You have to think, and no one in this country can forget, that Australia began as a penal colony. There was a huge anxiety amongst the people themselves and amidst those who governed them about the whole notion of the 'convict seed'. Could you have a decent society? Could you breed from this stock and have something worthwhile? And people – I think often of my parents even, certainly my grandparents' generation – there's a sort of sense of shame about this, and there was this notion of the convict stain.

Carey left to travel when he was twenty-four. Nearly forty years later, he would remember that arriving in England felt '*reeeally* good', the pleasure still resonant in his voice. 'The immigration guy looked at me and he said, "You look more English than the English." I felt really pleased.

Everything about coming here really felt like coming home,' he told the BBC. 'I had long hair which made me, at that time in Australia, a possible victim of a beating at any moment. And suddenly it felt really safe to be here, to live in Notting Hill. I felt deeply, deeply at home.'

*

Formal training gives you an armoury of named techniques. Its absence gives you the ignorance and impetus to white-knuckle it through the discovery of other ways in. It may be accurate to say that those of us who lack formal training – when we take the training wheels off and wobble past influence – are led, for the first books at least, by intuition. The right word, or image; where it goes in relation to others to hit the right note or rhythm.

There is deep pleasure in executing 'weird sentences and nice images and all those sorts of things', as Carey once put it.[31] For me, the best thing that occurs when writing is not when words seemingly write themselves, which happens so rarely that you forget it happens at all. The best thing is when you finally find something that clicks. A detail, a passage, a consciousness – your voice. Sublime. Carey is excellent at this. To be this excellent at finding where something belongs, you have to be expert at not just knowing but feeling where it doesn't.

Carey has characterised an important part of his work as 'a slightly peripheral or colonial or post-colonial viewpoint', with 'the objective to make the imperial centre see the periphery and understand what the fuck it's doing to people'.

'It's baffling to hear Carey still speaking from the periphery,' Susan Wyndham wrote in a profile in 2006. 'He is the author of 16 books, winner of two Booker Prizes and two Commonwealth Writers' Prizes. He has lived in Manhattan – the centre of the centre – since 1990. Since 2002 he has had dual Australian–US citizenship. He's rich and well-connected, ambitious and proud. Yet he carries a whiff of the Aussie underdog who got away with it – so far.' Here, in Wyndham's bafflement, we get closer to the marrow.

Carey is forever returning to outsiders, the abject, that which 'disturb[s] identity, system, and order'.[32] Maggs's scar tissue. Lucinda's curls escaping their pin. Oscar's creaking knees. Theophilus Hopkins' annihilating rage. Religious sentiment on stolen land. His elation about that British immigration officer's approval. The great distance between close generations, and between people and the reality of their history, in the country where he was born. Wyndham was right – it is true that in a nation not known for its justice, the 'convict stain' never was, materially or emotionally, a primary wrong. It is also true that internalised shame cannot be healed with work or prizes or planes or sales or the march of time.

*

'If there's a prettier war memorial than our Avenue of Honour, I never heard of it,' says Irene in *A Long Way from Home*, of Bacchus Marsh. In a certain light, more an angle of vision than of the sun, it all dematerialises: the cars and trucks ahead of me squeezing themselves around the small roundabout, the KFC, the McDonald's, the pizza places, until the quiet country town appears as it was in the 1940s, when it could've gone differently – the direction in which we channelled all that endurance, that sheer force of will. Housing, health, education, definitely. From there, perhaps, immigration, individuation, treaty as we finally confronted, and mourned, our true beginnings. We are, after all, not incapable of grief or memory. 'Every tree in the avenue was planted for a local boy that died. Every trunk had its own name. The dead boys are now huge elms and they join together above the road and give a very calm impression.' I'm driving under those dead boys now, their branches forming a canopy above me, trying to hold in my mind the town that shaped Carey.

Across his books, there is a thick concern with the stories that shape us, personally and collectively. All those things which, for better or worse, 'are like the dark marks made in the rings of great trees locked forever in our daily selves'.[33] I see the school on Lerderderg Street, the roof of the original building crenellated like icing on a gingerbread house. The building that housed Carey Motors, the windows of the apartment upstairs where he lived as a child. The vast space all around.

The light is so bright that I need to squint through my sunnies as I approach the highway back to Melbourne. The clouds are still riding low over those long plains which John Batman described in 1835 as so vast and fictionally vacant that '[f]ive thousand sheep would be almost lost upon them'. By 1842, pastoral occupation of the shire was complete, the Murnong roots and kangaroo grass steadily vanishing as select sons grew transcendentally wealthy from meeting the parent country's desires. I wait for a gap in the unending stream of traffic, take my chance when it comes, speeding past a dead kangaroo on the shoulder of that dirty highway, its fur blown back by the wind.

III

What do we keep? What do we carry? As a boy, Ned Kelly risked his life to save a privileged class-mate, Dick Shelton, from drowning in a flooded creek and was rewarded with a green silk sash. 'I looked down at my person,' Carey's Kelly says, 'and seen not my bare feet my darned pullover my patched pants but a 7 ft. sash. It were pea-cock green embroidered with gold TO EDWARD KELLY IN GRATITUDE FOR HIS COURAGE FROM THE SHELTON FAMILY.' That sash is displayed at the Costume and Kelly Museum in Benalla. You can see bloodstains on it. Kelly was wearing it under his armour when he was shot by police and arrested at Glenrowan.

The author and (at the time) fellow copywriter Barry Oakley took Carey to see Nolan's Kelly series at Georges' Art Gallery on Collins Street. 'It was 1964,' Carey later wrote,

around the time when Gabriel García Márquez was writing: 'The world was so recent that many things lacked names, and in order to indicate them it was necessary to point.' I was 21. All of art was new to me and nothing was not interesting …

Now I obsessed about Nolan, followed my nose from his paintings to the letter Kelly had written in 1879 before he robbed the bank in Jerilderie … You can Google it these days. Please do. I hope you see what I saw: Ned Kelly is on fire … I had written one unpublished story but was not shy to think that I might write a novel that would transform everyone's idea of that bearded Australian bushranger … I did not fix the spelling. I did not add a comma. I transcribed the letter and carried it on my person like a holy cross.[34]

If it seems bizarre to you that a 21-year-old would carry on his person (for a time, anyway, before he lost it at a pub) the 7389-word document Kelly had described as his autobiography[35] – consider that green sash. And our truest homes, which are kept beneath our armour, close to the skin.

No transformative bushranger novel materialised for another thirty years. And then it is 1994. The Metropolitan Museum of Art is showing Nolan's Ned Kelly series from 19 April to 4 September. I imagine Carey taking the train uptown from his home in the Village after a morning of writing, walking towards the museum through the park along the neat lines laid by Vaux and Olmsted, canopied, in those warm months, by elm trees. A flash of annoyance at the summer hordes swamping the front steps. He parts ways with them as they dutifully dart towards the mummies or the Impressionists. And then he is in the cool, quiet room with the Kellys, surprised by a stab of homesickness.

Or maybe it goes like this: the room with the Kellys in that American temple of art and memory is busy with curious visitors. He is intrigued by the audience's attention, feels a pang of the proprietary, and an urgency born of the ad man's sense of what will sell ... Perhaps. I don't buy it, though, because, for better or worse, certain writers write the books they are ineluctably called to write. The primary motive of art-making – passion sustained over years of meticulous labour – is as simple and as complex as that. 'One by one, I brought my new Manhattan friends uptown and walked them around the 27 paintings as if they were the stations of the cross,' he continued, about the drive *to tell* that signifies the start of such a book. 'I explained why, while we had no Thomas Jefferson, our imaginary founding father was a convicted murderer named Ned Kelly.'

In the exhibition catalogue, I read – as Carey might have – the essay by Andrew Sayers. He writes,

Much of Nolan's early work engaged with the possibilities and limitations of the visual and the verbal – the tension between what can be done with paint and what can be done only with the temporal and rhythmic medium of words. As a young man, Nolan could not decide whether to be a painter or a poet. In the Kelly series, narrative – having rhythm and passage over time – brought these two tendencies together. Yet somehow the disjunctive, episodic nature of the Kelly paintings denies any fluidity of 'reading'.

From another angle, though, it might be precisely this disjunctive, episodic quality that – like any novel or film – *creates* the possibility of reading. Unlike the continuous river of time containing all the undifferentiated details of life, storytelling is selective, partial, incomplete. The audience reflexively fills in gaps with its own understandings, projections and longings until what is episodic or fragmentary moves in the mind as fluidly as blood. And no matter how completely a thesis is articulated – how bluntly it conveys an 'instant sensory awareness' of the intended whole[36] – the audience will make their own meanings of it. All narratives are relational, each 'pend[ing] completion in other eyes, mind, and hearts'.[37]

Seeing Nolan's paintings against the utterly strange backdrop of Fifth Avenue freed something in Carey. Perhaps it released him from the gaps punctuating the chronology of Kelly's life and the frustrating partisanship of great swathes of Kelly scholarship, so much of which boils down to word-on-word; what was anathema for the historian could be manna for the novelist. Carey was now twice as old as that kid who'd walked around with the Jerilderie Letter in his pocket. He had four novels, a Booker shortlisting, a Booker win and two Miles Franklin Awards to his name. He was working on the draft of *Jack Maggs*, had hidden histories and the convict stain on the brain, as well as returning and rumination as responses to the traumas of abandonment and abuse. He was in command of his craft and solidly at home 16,500 kilometres from home. Which is all to say that in that many-windowed temple full of hallways and doors, 'the sort of place where you are always arriving where you do not expect',[38] he finally found a way in.

*

True History argues from its Faulknerian epigraph to its last gasp that 'The past is not dead. It is not even past.'

*

Everyone is accounted for in that world-building first chapter. The colony in microcosm: anvil-hooved cattle 'flooding down the smooth green hill of Beveridge like a breaking wave', the squatter's bull worth five times everything the Kelly family owns. The Frontier Wars, Aboriginal warriors resisting the apocalyptic violence of their dispossession. The downward remove at which the Protestant establishment kept the Catholic poor, like the Kellys. The brutalised Irish convicts' fear and rage towards the poorly trained, poorly supervised Irish ranks of Victoria Police who could destroy a life, a family, in a matter of seconds. The dirt-poor Irish-Catholics trying to conjure something sustaining from rocks and mud or dust on windy hillsides. The full hierarchy of countrymen who were divided by factors so flimsy that they required a ruthless vigilance.

Before the Crown enforced a system of tenure in its own interests, things were not so orderly. Of the original land grab, barrister John Quick wrote in 1883:

> The early squatters of Australia … took up vast territories of unoccupied land as large as German principalities, which they possessed for many years with very considerable

advantage to themselves ... When a new district is opened by some enterprising colonists, there is a general rush for runs. The first comer takes a bird's eye view of an extensive and well-watered valley and, without any reference to the extent required for his stock, he says: 'This is my run.' The next follows his example, and, in a short time, the whole district is parcelled out.[39]

Subsequent sons, grandiose misfits, enterprising ticket-of-leave convicts whom the Crown had absolved itself from feeding – everyone untethered from the holding environments of their rightful home places, and striving to acquire more, faster, than those old countries were willing to give. The ghosts who may still be heard.

'Your grandfather were a quiet and secret man he had been ripped from his home in Tipperary and transported to the prisons of Van Diemen's Land I do not know what was done to him he never spoke of it. When they had finished with their tortures they set him free and he crossed the sea to the colony of Victoria.' The novel starts with exquisite tenderness and exquisite violence. A father writing to his baby daughter, unable to contemplate the possibility that the feudal injustices of his day would poison hers, too. 'How queer and foreign it must seem to you and all the coarse words and cruelty which I now relate are far away in ancient time.' And yet he would be torn from his child, as his father was torn from him.

The quality of Carey's attention is such that he sees doubly. The past in the present. The 'unguarded, open-faced' child in the adult.[40] The lies in the official narratives – national ones, family ones, personal ones. He is an archaeologist, expert at where to dig and when to brush at the sediment to reveal that once-beating heart frozen in rock. This is why he begins with the devastating detail that despite the scarcity and danger, it was all normal to the child: 'I lived at Pleurisy Plains.

I could not conceive a better soil or prettier view or trees that did not grow crooked in the winds.'

*

Ned's father, like that parent country which ruined him, was 'a man of secrets and what he said and done was different things'. Frequently, the parents Carey draws cannot, or do not, keep their children safe, emotionally or otherwise. They are cold spaces, 'with nothing bright or soft or sympathetic'.[41] Like Red Kelly, many of the fathers are bullies or hollowed out by their own woundings: Theophilus Hopkins, Dan Bobs, Herbert Badgery's bad dad, 'as cold to his children as he was charming to his customers ... never show[ing] his anger to the men who had caused it ... but only to his family',[42] Tobias Oates' father, who cannot be remembered without bitterness. Young Ned has the same qualities as dutiful little Jack Maggs and motherless Oscar Hopkins – hypervigilant, 'a useful little chap, as if [his] life depended on it',[43] attention and sympathy trained to flow only upward.[44]

In a child's mind, the norm of a neglectful or cruel parent will be split off from consciousness in order to create the illusion of safety. Self-blame, or simple confusion, are used to conceal frightening parental behaviour and preserve the fiction of unconditional love.[45] When such children – young Ned, Oscar, Herbert – finally wrench themselves away from their indifferent or explosive fathers, that once-adaptive self-loathing persists, continuing to unground them. There is nowhere for these grown men to direct their rightful rage but inwards or onto others: 'The anger was unthinkable, but it was not a thinking thing.'[46] Chronic anger or compulsive behaviour – lying, gambling, working – is the lot of such not-truly-individuated children after they become adults. 'Many is the night I have sat by the roaring river the rain never ending them logs so green bubbling and spitting blazing in a rage no rain can staunch.'[47]

Across the novels, the mothers are typically more capable. But, like Ellen Kelly and Ma Britten and Mercy Larkin's mother, they betray their children by entrusting them to criminals, trading their safety for money. Or, like Elizabeth Leplastrier or Oscar's or Jack's or Herbert's or Felix Moore's mum, they vanish altogether. Frequently, the mothers are under-supported by the fathers, so alone and beaten down that they 'cannot feel' their children clinging to them, kissing them.[48]

Effectively alone, these children learn to trust themselves too much or too little – resolving their 'torture of confusion' by unseeing what is in front of them, or inside them.[49] So the mistreated son cries out for his Da. Or hugs the mum who 'bought and sold [him] like carrion', thinking 'how deep I loved her we was grown together like 2 branches of an old wisteria'. Psychologically, that is how it goes – it is not uncommon for the most painful parents to inspire the fiercest, most defensively idealising devotion.

*

True History comes armoured by archives: the story spools out across parcels containing Kelly's letter, complete with appendices and accession numbers, from the centre of the Melbourne Public Library (now State Library Victoria). With this mix of real and imagined, Carey found new ways of making emotionally visible the weft of the present around the warp of the past.

Typically, a Carey novel is poly-vocal, short-chaptered, the complex human whole gestured towards through competing consciousnesses. *True History*, however, is mostly Ned's voice; its chapters are longer, as are its lightly punctuated sentences. In its rhetorical register it mirrors the Jerilderie Letter, which combines laughter and rage and lyricism. That letter is often described as a PR stunt by Kelly, an attempt at self-promotion. Maybe. It does, however, have the quicksand quality of abuse disclosure – the injustice so clear and appalling that starting with any one incident or detail is beside the point, and yet one has to start some-where. Reading it, there is a strong sense that he was 'hurt into poetry', as Yeats put it, though less by 'Mad Ireland' and more by the colony which continued to enact on its Irish-Catholics the pre-judices of England at every turn. Its crudely crafted sentences carry the reader along currents of feeling; it reads like few other historical documents. This is because we continue to be its intended audience, and its concerns are not yet closed.

Sidney Nolan thought that the Kelly story could 'be called one of our Australian myths'. Professor Ross Gibson has explained that myths highlight contradictions we feel compelled to resolve narratively rather than rationally, so that we can get on with living. 'Myths help us live with contradictions, whereas histories help us analyse persistent contradictions so that we might avoid being lulled and ruled by the myths that we use to console and enable ourselves. Which is why we desire our myths and need our histories.'[50]

The draft title of the novel was *The Secret History of the Kelly Gang* – a homage to the first major book on Kelly, J.J. Kenneally's *The Inner History of the Kelly Gang*. Both titles live inside the finished book because the truest history *is* the secret one, the inner one – the emotional one. Which means that, in Australia, it is also the impossible one, because externalising such things requires extreme vulnerability. Had that quality been available to men like Ned Kelly, they would never have lived long enough to tell their tales.

*

Three days before the nation voted on the republic referendum in November 1999, playwright David Williamson sent Carey his thoughts on the last draft of the book, 'literally seconds' after reading the final page.

> Usually your central character is someone we empathise with. Someone who has suffered

undeserved misfortune, but Ned is the most vital of all these. You feel with him the grim oppression of struggling to make a living in impossible conditions. All the hard toil in the world is not going to help one of those small selectors ever make a go of it in a country that is subject to El Niño drought and flood and whose soils need thousands of acres to make grazing and agriculture possible, and those large holdings had already been grabbed by the English squatters. The sheer oppressive impossibility of it all generates huge sympathy for Ned and we admire his courage and resilience in refusing to accept his fate when the cards have been so obviously stacked against him. We admire him for realising so astutely just how cunningly the apparatus of state has been deployed against him and admire his rage at the sheer UNFAIRNESS of it all.

The hatred of unfairness is both a universal and a very Australian thing. In Australia it is amplified because the unfairness was just so obvious, so you have captured, from your New York eyrie an essential part of us. I have never really been able to get a sense of the genesis of the Kelly phenomena until I read your book. Telling the story from his viewpoint in his voice made his whole world available to us and we UNDERSTAND, in the very best sense. The courage and toughness, the pride and concern for reputation, the belief, touching, if deluded, that he could lead an uprising against unfairness in his fiefdom …

To be cut off from one's culture in a forbidding and unforgiving new world is a special type of horror … I feel I now understand my heritage a whole lot better than I did before I read your book, which is a lot more than straight history has ever done for me.

*

Carey's 'ventriloquism' is often mentioned,[51] but when it comes to voice he's more superb than the lyrebird – he's a bowerbird. Collecting, collaging. What might have been the hardest aspect of writing *True History* – replicating and sustaining Kelly's voice – came naturally. As Carey has explained, the sound of his schoolyard is in that language. The vernacular of both *True History* and the Jerilderie Letter reads quaintly to a great swathe of the book's readers. But elements of it persist in many neighbourhoods and environments: the lower courts, the commission flats, the underfunded schools in underfunded rural and regional towns. Places no Grammarian usually goes. Despite these continuities, in the end, as Ramona Koval observed, Kelly was 'a revolutionary without a revolution'. No uprising occurred; a royal remains our head of state. *True History* goes some way towards illuminating why that is unsurprising.

Dangerous hypocrisy – the barbarity bubbling beneath the cool surfaces of civility – is a constant in the worlds built by Carey. In *True History*, it presents as a social order bent around propitiating those in charge of, and favoured by, the colonial administration. 'And here is the thing about them men,' Carey's Kelly explains. 'They knew full well the terror of the unyielding law the historic moment of UNFAIRNESS were in their blood and a man might be a bank clerk or an overseer he might never have been lagged for nothing but still he knew in his heart what it were to be forced to wear the white hood in prison he knew what it were to be lashed for looking a warder in the eye.'

*

In a 2013 issue of *Quadrant*, Peter Ryan reviewed Ian MacFarlane's *The Kelly Gang Unmasked*, writing with a noteworthy animus.

With MacFarlane … we have the necessary armamentarium to set to flight the current gushing fictions of the Left. ('Kelly Deniers', we shall probably be called.) Meanwhile they now speak of Ned's 'martyrdom' – yes, actually using that word. This necessary piece of basic national house-cleaning should come before all the now-looming frivolities of sacking the Queen, starting a republic, twiddling with the Constitution and inventing a new flag.

Then the tone shifted:

One quiet afternoon, over a brandy, the writer Cyril Pearl and I chatted to regal Mrs Davenport, presiding barmaid at the Hotel Windsor's grand saloon bar. She confided to us that she was the grand-daughter of Mounted Constable P.C. Gascoigne, one of the most active of the Kelly hunters, who had exchanged more than one angry shot with the Gang. She had inherited some of his reports, which she offered to bring in for us to read. Next day she handed us a well-worn brown leather 'sabretache', that rolled-up carry-case which hangs from the near (left) side of a cavalryman's saddle. 'Take it home for a few days, and read it at your leisure,' she said. And away we walked with a sheaf of reports, quillpenned on the final Ned Kelly battlefront, rolled in an old sabretache certainly imbued with the smoke of Glenrowan.

That smoke, and '(left)', those shared confidences – all mean proximity, authority, ownership. When it comes to the protagonists of the Kelly story – the cops or the crims – we've never stopped gazing at them like mirrors, needing to choose sides. Wanting, somehow, to be part of the band.

*

In Jung's hands, the concept of individuation referred to the difficult psychological process of actively discovering and becoming our true selves.[52] 'One cannot individuate as long as one is playing a role to oneself,' he said, explaining that the capitulations we make at the service of social acceptance are 'the most subtle obstacle against true individuation'. The consequences of identifying with those masks we learn to wear are life-constricting: an estrangement from one's self and sense of purpose and meaning, as well as the ability to truly connect with others. But one always has the choice of finding and then learning to live 'out of one's own centre, in control of one's for and against'.[53]

The process is not without its costs. 'It is a most painful procedure to tear off those veils, but each step forward in psychological development means just that, the tearing off of a new veil. We are like onions with many skins, and we have to peel ourselves again and again in order to get at the real core.'[54]

*

At the time of his email to Carey, Williamson was writing an op-ed for *The Sydney Morning Herald* about the imminent republic referendum: '[A]lthough this isn't an election night it feels to me like a very important evening in the history of our nation. This feeling doesn't seem to be widely shared. "Waste of time and money" is a common response I've been getting. "Who gives a stuff?" is another. "How's it going to change my life?" is a third. Yet when people say this, there's something about the manner in which it's said that gives me pause. A jut of the chin, a furrowed brow, hints of anger lying just below the surface.'[55]

'The referendum does mean something to most of these people,' Williamson continued. 'What they're really telling me is that they're going to vote "no". Not for the reasons they've stated, not even because they dislike the proposed model, but for reasons they won't articulate, because those reasons are emotional and they'd rather find spurious rational reasons than admit to that.'

One group of 'no' voters, he explained, was driven by contempt for the politicians set to gain from it, who had shown them little consideration in 'ruthless and highly competitive times [where] societies' winners are becoming even bigger winners and the rest are having their noses increasingly rubbed in their relative failure'.

'The second group of hugely emotional "no" voters are our avowed monarchists,' Williamson continued. 'And the change that frightens and disturbs them is the change in our ethnic composition … The Queen is obviously not a foreigner to them. In their hearts she is what they are. British.

'In trying to understand this I remember … my father proudly telling me that his good friend George, a fellow banker of Greek extraction, hauled a recalcitrant up by his shoulders in the cinema when this despicable creature refused to stand for God Save the Queen … By this act he had, in my father's eyes, proved himself "one of us". Not Australian, but "British". What my father didn't realise, as he'd never been there, was that the real "British" didn't see us as British at all ... the real English patronised us at best, and despised us at worst.'

This reminded me of the memory Carey gave to *Illywhacker*'s Herbert Badgery: 'This story concerns my father who I always imagined to be an Englishman, who made such a thing, as long as I knew him, of his Englishness, who never missed a chance to say, "I am an Englishman" or, "as an Englishman" that I was surprised to find out he was born in York Street, Warrnambool, the son of a shopkeeper. Yet for all that, I must carry his lie for him. For he made himself into an Englishman and my first memory of him is being chastised for the way I spoke.'

*

Anybody can be angry, that's easy, Aristotle said a couple of millennia ago, 'but to be angry with the right person, and to the right degree, and at the right time, and for the right purpose, and in the right way, that is not within everybody's power, that is not easy.'[56]

IV

State Library Victoria is Australia's oldest public library and one of the world's first free libraries. It opened in 1856 to anyone over fourteen who could demonstrate that they had clean hands. In the forecourt, in front of the stairs that Nolan would climb to read Rilke and Rimbaud, Redmond Barry stands between St George and Joan of Arc: 'ERECTED BY A GRATEFUL PUBLIC TO PERPETUATE THE MEMORY OF INVALUABLE SERVICES RENDERED TO VICTORIA BY SIR REDMOND BARRY DOCTOR OF LAWS AND A JUDGE OF THE SUPREME COURT'.

We are selective with perpetual memory, as we are with our definition of 'clean hands', and whom we take to be our judges. But sometimes that works in unintended ways. Barry's memory will be forever tied to Kelly, whom he sentenced to die and whose postpartum mother he had previously sentenced to three years' hard labour.

'I am a Widow's Son, outlawed and my orders must be obeyed.' I had earlier spread out before me the petite pages of the Jerilderie Letter – as yellowed and delicate as potato chips – in their plastic pockets. They were then restored to their bespoke green archival box, which I am pushing in a metal trolley through back corridors of the library like a baby in a pram. In front of me is an archivist pushing drafts of Carey's *True History* in white-grey archival boxes, the colour of ghost gums. After returning the letter to its safe, we walk the other materials silently down the length of the Herald and Weekly Times Newspapers Reading Room, which ends in an atrium where Kelly's bullet-dented armour stands in a display case like a disembodied knight.

When Carey wrote *True History*, the library had not yet acquired the Jerilderie Letter. Now both the letter and the drafts of the book – a fictionalised version of that letter kept in that library – have made their home in the actual building. Before I open the Carey boxes, a library employee tells me about the ghosts said to haunt these halls. But they are not the ghosts I am immediately concerned with.

In the quiet room, with the light streaming through the window on my right and Kelly's bullet-dented helmet through the glass door on my left, I trace the course of Carey's creation. It is unexpectedly moving to pick up his typed chronology of events. Its red plastic paperclip is not so different from the metal one that once held together the Jerilderie pages, which will bear the indent of that tight and rusted coil until they disintegrate entirely.

Interestingly, early drafts open with Kelly berating himself for his failures towards his father, displacing the pain of that stunted relationship into a busily self-castigating narrative rather than the truer, but more initially devastating, one of unmet need and longing. Kelly's voice in its fullest flight does not emerge until the final draft. Once the book's architecture was solid, tiny adjustments at the sentence level had the sublime effect of refracting light. The narrative consciousness of the book – Ned's – became less a voice that could've belonged to Jack Maggs the faux footman, or a workman in Lucinda's factory, and became itself only. As the drafts progress, the pages of explanatory framing vanish, Ned's symptomatic self-flagellation disappears, his grammar subsides, punctuation attenuates and the lyrical darlings are killed, until Carey's Kelly seems to stride out from the page, refusing to betray himself – or his younger self – and I have to close my burning eyes in that streaming light for an unexpectedly long moment.

Visiting the Met with his American mates, during those warm months when Nolan's paintings hung in its cool rooms, Carey was refining his explanation, above all to himself, why a grandiose, cop-killing horse thief remains locked in our collective consciousness, occupying space usually reserved for statesmen or war heroes. In Kelly, a not insubstantial portion of the nation recognises two magnetising archetypes, the outlaw and the hero, and in those minds the two images are not dissociable.

Neither is the nation itself dissociable from the atrocities integral to its founding, and the inequalities that we have allowed to persist. Here, no police officer has ever been held accountable by the criminal law for any of the tens of thousands of Aboriginal people who have died at their hands or in their custody.[57] Here, one in six children live in poverty.[58] Over half of food-insecure households have someone in paid work, employment no longer functioning as a shield against hunger.[59] In 2022, the United Nations Committee Against Torture listed urgent concerns about our sustained, punitive treatment of asylum seekers: 'mandatory detention, including for children, overcrowding, inadequate healthcare … assault, sexual abuse, self-harm, ill-treatment and suspicious deaths'.[60] Born with access to less because 'the so-called legal owners' had already brutally stolen more for themselves,[61] the fascination with Kelly may be the closest that large swathes of White Australia have come to acknowledging the reality that has always been self-evident to Indigenous communities: the lie in the very name of the Commonwealth.

It's an unlikely mix, those who want to be part of Kelly's band: anti-vaxxers, a whisky company, the bikies who stop by his unmarked grave, artists, writers and the constant stream of visitors silently gazing for prolonged periods at his pocked helmet in the display case. But perhaps it is true to say that for those who once needed protection that never came – and can no longer find it in themselves to mask their learned unworthiness by identifying with their oppressor – there will be some part drawn to Kelly as a symbol of righteous defiance against unjust authority.

I bury the manuscripts back in their boxes, pack my bag. Retrace my steps through the belly of the building I first visited shortly after moving here, still just a kid, back when it housed the Melbourne Museum's dinosaurs and big cats frozen mid-roar. This is where, as a uni student, I choose topics for my history assignments with the express purpose of researching under the dome. In the cafe, my husband and I celebrated our engagement. In this building, I am only ever a younger age, looking at the layers of Marvellous Melbourne, and myself.

I go down the front steps, where the sun paints the students and young people moving everywhere in pairs and groups, none of their combinations Anglo only. Clanging trams are swallowed down Swanston Street, where they will pass Hamer Hall and the state funeral for Uncle Jack Charles underway at this moment. I wait for the lights to change, standing near Spronk's bluestone *Architectural Fragment*, that replicated frontal corner of the library, column and architrave sinking into the sidewalk 'like a lost civilisation'.[62] After two years of isolation – during which the city was so vacant that Spronk's comment lost any irony – the details are overwhelming. A street preacher is barking about the messiah, the new Jerusalem. In front of Melbourne Central a man is begging outside a bakery, his forehead nearly touching a dingy little plaque embedded in the footpath: QUEEN ELIZABETH PLAZA NAMED BY HER MAJESTY THE QUEEN 28 MAY 1980.

*

For those who have endured prolonged dismissal or denial, simple evidence that the past happened is endlessly enthralling, holy. In one of Carey's files is a photocopy of an extraordinarily disturbing photo, misattributed and misidentified by the institution that provided it. 'Description: NED KELLY, HUNGOUTSIDE MAELBOURNE JAILE, KRUGER FRED'. Taken in 1880, after the siege at

Glenrowan, it is a photo of a photo being taken of 23-year-old Joe Byrne, his heels dangling just above the ground below his singed and lifeless body, which is strung up, like a marionette, on the door of the Benalla gaol.

In front of Byrne, a photographer is poised behind a tripod, head under black cloth. Behind him stand five men. One is in shirtsleeves and an Akubra-style hat, casually thumbing his nose. The others wear bowlers and suits of dark materials. All of them are as nonchalant as Kelly would be when Barry sentenced him to hang months later. Also in the photo: three boys. The face of the littlest child is blurred by the motion of his head looking back over his shoulder. Imagine his interior weather. This image of the dominated dead is Australia's 'first ever press photograph'.[63]

Geoffrey Serle once wrote that the Kelly gang were 'the last expression of the lawless frontier in what was becoming a highly organised and educated society, the last protest of the mighty bush now tethered with iron rails to Melbourne and the world'.[64] After his trial, at which he was inadequately represented by counsel, Kelly was hanged away from public view.[65] Barry died twelve days later, didn't live to see publicised what he would've already known through his work and his mates at the Melbourne Club. In 1883, the report of the Royal Commission on the Police Force of Victoria laid out the corrupt and inefficient administration of the police department.[66] Commissioner Frederick Charles Standish, under whose sloppy and corrupt oversight much of the hunt for the Kellys was conducted, was found to have been responsible for police operations that were 'not characterized either by good judgment, or by that zeal for the interests of the public service which should have distinguished an officer in his position'. As Gough Whitlam put it, when recommending Alex C. Castles' legal history, *Ned Kelly's Last Days*: 'there were malefactors at many levels in the colony of Victoria'. From this perspective, then, it is more accurate to say that the Kelly gang were the last *public* expression of the lawless frontier, in what was becoming a highly organised and educated society which preferred plausible deniability when it came to its sustaining violences. Civility demanded such things become unavailable to the eye.

*

'The violence from which the paintings sprang and which they originally embodied for the artist and for those around him became less apparent over time,' wrote Andrew Sayers, in the 1994 Met catalogue. 'Nolan observed in the 1980s that the paintings seemed to have become less angry and more lyrical. For the audience, too, the force of feeling is harder and harder to recover.' That audience is used to one place being called the past and another the present.

Today, this audience can rent 'for various corporate functions' the building where Ellen Kelly did laundry while her son was hanged and 'engage with authentic historical figures such as Ned Kelly, Gaol Governors and roaming Police Sergeants'. Pentridge – where boys and young men were gaoled and raped – is a cinema, Ararat's lunatic asylum is a viticulture college and the bluestone markers from the old gaolyard graves are now zipped past daily by old boys in their foreign cars, driving along the stone seawall lining the bay. As Hilary Mantel wrote in her memoir *Giving Up the Ghost*, 'You search for [history] in the same way you sift through a landfill: for evidence of what people want to bury.'

Fiction and non-fiction are both ways of working with what the earth gives us to arrive at human truths. But while fiction is spacious enough for quantum complexities – mixing what is factually true with what is factually false at the service of ecstatic truth – history is an unforgiving medium where one cannot have it both ways. No inventions, no distortions, no 'I' that is equally not.

This unaccommodating reality is perhaps why, as a country, we have embraced our history in its fullness only in the form of fiction, and why – as things currently stand – our appetite for that particular sort of book will never be sated.

In vital ways, Australia is still that place where you can only be the happy camper or the kid weeping in the corner. To speak directly about the blazingly obvious – that certain prosperities are rooted in emotional and material poverty – is to shift the paradigms of public, and institutional, life barely at all. Standing on the corner of La Trobe and Swanston, I try to see that shaky isosceles again. The library, the old art school, the old court. Nolan passing the bronze judge on his way to read poetry in the building where Kelly's helmet and the laptop on which Carey wrote about its forging from ploughshares now remain in the dark when the lights go off. But the image will not hold amid the barking and the clanging, the traffic and the timetable loading too slowly on my phone.

When I look up again, it's just the library, just the RMIT buildings and, around the corner, that dark place where the state that cares so reverentially for Kelly's property once snapped his neck.

I am thinking about the phrase 'more English than the English', and how in certain relationships we haemorrhage parts of ourselves in an effort to be loved, repeatedly locating our sense of safety where there is, and will be, none.

I am thinking of that boy who wasn't at home in the school where students were called by their surnames but whose time there meant that he was no longer at home in the town where boys left school at fourteen, had their teeth pulled for a quid and went to work in the mines. The young man who wasn't at home in the pubs where everyone had a degree or where no one had a degree. I am thinking of his mother, who completed one year in a private academy, of his father in a freezing field needing to close a sale, and the weight of what Jung called our parents' unlived lives. The tidal waves of change from frontier to federation, Boer War to Vietnam, and how they barely disturbed the sediment of submerged cultural fears and values and woundings. I am thinking of the extraordinary conflicts all this would've created in developing minds sensitive to their environments.

Truth is the friend of originality and, in turn, new forms of human connection. By following it, the artist ends up, as Nolan said, 'with a landscape one has never seen before but it is presumably the landscape you were feeling as you started'. In formally representing their interior terrain, Nolan and Carey – like Kelly – did something therapeutic for the nation and entered the canon of Western art. But you don't have to look many generations back before you see that certain young men marked themselves out by their close concern for memory, emotion and communication. Islands on an island, chilled by 'the perfect coldness known to climbers'.[67]

Nolan and Carey – who found new uses for

the old materials of inferiority, internalised shame and subordination – were not so different to the 'currency lads', those earliest native-born settlers 'left alone ignorant as tadpoles spawned in puddles on the moon'. This was not only in the sense of having no local artistic forebears, although that too is probably true. I am referring to the solitary battle each fought, caught in a double bind between their material, which remained here, and their homes, which they made elsewhere, doomed to re-enact the tyrannies of distance.

Nolan moved to England, where he was knighted in 1981. He's buried in Highgate cemetery. Carey became a US citizen in 2002, receiving the Carnegie Corporation of New York's Great Immigrant Award in 2021. Sometimes, that's the cost of refusing the false histories: if you look at certain things directly, you might never again make it home.

ACKNOWLEDGEMENTS

I am grateful to Peter Carey for his work. Thank you to Chris Feik, Rebecca Bauert, Jane Novak, Quincy Scavron Orr and the librarians and archivists at the magnificent State Library Victoria for their illuminating expertise, generosity and good counsel. Gratitude also to Michael Williams, who got me to crack open that first book. And to Charlie, always.

NOTES

1   Quoted in Isabella Boorman, 'Ern Malley (Self-Portrait), 1973', Sidney Nolan Trust, https://sidneynolantrust.org/nolan-100/ern-malley-self-portrait-45.

2   Peter Ryan, *Redmond Barry: A Colonial Life 1813–1880*, second edition, Melbourne University Press, Carlton, 1980, p. 2.

3   Geoffrey Smith, 'Nolan's Vision', *The Age*, 31 May 2003.

4   *Weekly Times* (Melbourne), 9 October 1946.

5   Sidney Nolan's letter to John Reed, Brisbane, 10 July 1947, Reed Papers, State Library Victoria.

6   Printed as 'The Unexamined Life', *Meanjin*, vol. 56, no. 4, 1997.

7   Quoted in *Sidney Nolan's Ned Kelly*, National Gallery of Australia, 2002.

8   *Oscar & Lucinda*, p. 373.

9   Patrick Allington, 'Conversation with Peter Carey', *Kill Your Darlings*, no. 20, 8 January 2015.

10   W.G. Sebald, 'Across the Border: Peter Handke's *Repetition*', 1995, translated by Nathanial Davis, The Last Books, 2013.

11   Quoted in Mel Gussow, 'Championing a Fabled Bandit; for Novelist, a Rogue Australian Sums

Up His Underdog Culture', *The New York Times*, 15 February 2001.

12   Quoted in Elwyn Lynn, *Sidney Nolan: Myth and Imagery*, MacMillan, London, 1967.

13   Radhika Jones, 'The Art of Fiction No. 188', *The Paris Review*, Issue 177, Summer 2006.

14   *Oscar & Lucinda*, pp. 136–37.

15   *Oscar & Lucinda*, p. 198.

16   *Amnesia*, p. 80.

17   *Jack Maggs*, Chapter 12.

18   *Oscar & Lucinda*, p. 372.

19   See David Naimon, Interview with Hélène Cixous, *Between the Covers* podcast.

20   Matthew Flinders, *A Voyage to Terra Australis*, vol. 1, 1814.

21   Magdalena Ball, Interview with Peter Carey, Compulsive Reader, 18 March 2003.

22   John Kelly, 'Such Is Life', *Art Monthly*, issue 258, April 2013, pp. 26, 28.

23   Robert McCrum, 'The 100 Best Novels: No 100 – *True History of the Kelly Gang* by Peter Carey (2000)', *The Guardian*, 16 August 2015.

24   *Oscar & Lucinda*, p. 395.

25   *Oscar & Lucinda*, pp. 210, 223.

26   *Oscar & Lucinda*, p. 395.

27   *Oscar & Lucinda*, p. 413.

28   Quoted in Miranda Stewart, 'Australian Stories of Tax and Fairness: A Feminist Reading of Peter Carey's *The*

Tax Inspector', *Australian Feminist Law Journal*, vol. 18, 2003; 'The Unexamined Life', *Meanjin*, vol. 56, no. 4, 1997; Patrick Allington, 'Conversation with Peter Carey', *Kill Your Darlings*, no. 20, 8 January 2015.

29   *Amnesia*, p. 7.

30   *Amnesia*, pp. 26, 29.

31   Allington, 'Conversation with Peter Carey'.

32   Julia Kristeva, *Powers of Horror: An Essay on Abjection*, Columbia University Press, New York, 1984; Ross Mitchell Guberman (ed.), *Julia Kristeva Interviews*, Columbia University Press, New York, 1996.

33   *True History of the Kelly Gang*, p. 19.

34   Peter Carey, 'Peter Carey on *True History of the Kelly Gang*: "At 56, I Wrote What My Younger Self Could Not Have Managed"', *The Guardian*, 8 February 2020.

35   See Alex C. Castles (with Jennifer Castles), *Ned Kelly's Last Days: Setting the Record Straight on the Death of an Outlaw*, Allen & Unwin, Sydney, 2005, p. 127.

36   Marshall McLuhan, *Understanding Media: The Extensions of Man*, McGraw-Hill, New York, 1964, p. 5.

37   Peter Schjeldahl, 'Young Rembrandt', *The New Yorker*, 1 August 2016.

38   *Oscar & Lucinda*, p. 203.

39   John Quick, 'The History of Land Tenure in the Colony of Victoria', *The Bendigo Independent* office, Sandhurst, 1883.

40   *Oscar & Lucinda*, p. 411.

41   *Oscar & Lucinda*, p. 425.

42   *Illywhacker*, p. 43.

43   *Jack Maggs*, Chapter 26.

44   *Illywhacker*, p. 12. ('In that odd household it was the
      parents who were the children ...', 'She watched her
      mother like a parent who knows a child will shortly
      stumble.'); *Oscar & Lucinda*, p. 45 ('Oscar looked up
      but was embarrassed by something in his father's eyes.
      The look was soft and pleading. It did not belong in
      that hard, black-bearded face, did not suit the tone of
      voice. Oscar knew this look. He had seen it before. It
      was a will-o'-the-wisp. If you tried to run towards it,
      it retreated; if you embraced it, it turned to distance in
      your arms. You could not hold it, that soft and lovely
      centre in his father's feelings.')

45   *Oscar & Lucinda*, p. 419. ('But if blame was a comm-
      odity like eggs or butter, he already had more than he
      could safely carry. And even while he prayed to God
      to ease his burden, he cast around for more to pick up
      and carry.')

46   *Oscar & Lucinda*, p. 23.

47   *True History of the Kelly Gang*, p. 186.

48   *True History of the Kelly Gang*, p. 7.

49   *True History of the Kelly Gang*, p. 13.

50   Ross Gibson, *Seven Versions of an Australian Badland*,
      University of Queensland Press, St Lucia, 2002, p. 171.

51   Craig Taylor, 'A High-Speed Auto Race Across
      Australia, Past and Present', *The New York Times*,
      14 March 2018.

52   Martin Schmidt, 'Individuation and the Self', Society of Analytical Psychology; C.G. Jung, 'Individuation', *Collected Works*, vol. 7, part 2, second edition, Princeton University Press, Princeton, 1966, p. 173ff.

53   Joseph Campbell, *Myths to Live By*, Viking, New York, 1972.

54   C.G. Jung, *Visions: Notes of the Seminar Given in 1930–1934*, Princeton University Press, Princeton, 1997.

55   David Williamson, 'Voting with a Vengeance', *The Sydney Morning Herald*, 6 November 1999.

56   Aristotle, *The Art of Rhetoric*, Penguin Classics, London, 1991.

57   See Russell Marks, 'Grim Territory', *The Monthly*, 15 September 2022.

58   Australia Council of Social Service, 'Poverty in Australia 2022: A Snapshot', Australian Council of Social Service and UNSW, Sydney, 2022.

59   Brianna Casey, 'Having a Job Is No Longer a Shield Against Poverty in Australia', *The Guardian*, 23 November 2022.

60   UN Committee Against Torture, 'Concluding Observations on the Sixth Periodic Report of Australia', 2022.

61   *Illywhacker*, p. 34. ('I left [my houses] to rot and rust and be shat on by cattle on the land of the so-called legal owners who were called squatters because they'd done exactly what I'd done.')

62 'Architectural Fragment', Visit Victoria, https://visitvictoria.com/regions/melbourne/ see-and-do/art-and-culture/public-art/ vv-architectural-fragment.

63 Rose Powell, 'First Australian Press Photo Shows Body of Kelly Gang Member Joe Byrne', *The Sydney Morning Herald*, 20 March 2015.

64 Geoffrey Serle, *The Rush to Be Rich: A History of the Colony of Victoria 1883–1889*, Melbourne University Press, Carlton, 1971, p. 11.

65 Castles, *Ned Kelly's Last Days*, p. xvii. ('I became convinced that regardless of whether the accused was guilty of his crimes or not – among them capital offences punishable by death – it could well be argued that according to the law at the time, Ned Kelly was tried, convicted and hanged *illegally*.')

66 Francis Longmore, *Royal Commission on the Police Force of Victoria*, Government Printer, Melbourne, 1883.

67 *Oscar & Lucinda*, p. 385.

BOOKS BY PETER CAREY

ADULT FICTION

Bliss (1981)

Illywhacker (1985)

Oscar & Lucinda (1988)

The Tax Inspector (1991)

The Unusual Life of Tristan Smith (1994)

Jack Maggs (1997)

True History of the Kelly Gang (2000)

My Life as a Fake (2003)

Theft: A Love Story (2006)

His Illegal Self (2008)

Parrot and Olivier in America (2009)

The Chemistry of Tears (2012)

Amnesia (2014)

A Long Way from Home (2017)

SHORT STORIES

The Fat Man in History (1974)

War Crimes (1979)

JUNIOR FICTION

The Big Bazoohley: A Story for Children (1995)

SCREENPLAYS

Bliss (1985, with Ray Lawrence)
Until the End of the World (1991,
with Wim Wenders)

STAGE

Illusion (1986, with Mike Mullins
and Martin Armiger)

NON-FICTION

A Letter to Our Son (1994)
30 Days in Sydney: A Wildly Distorted Account (2001)
Letter from New York (2001)
Wrong about Japan (2005)